# Growing Pains

## A Play

### Ian Armstrong

A SAMUEL FRENCH ACTING EDITION

SAMUEL FRENCH

FOUNDED 1830

SAMUELFRENCH-LONDON.CO.UK
SAMUELFRENCH.COM

Copyright © 1990 by Ian Armstrong
All Rights Reserved

*GROWING PAINS* is fully protected under the copyright laws of the British Commonwealth, including Canada, the United States of America, and all other countries of the Copyright Union. All rights, including professional and amateur stage productions, recitation, lecturing, public reading, motion picture, radio broadcasting, television and the rights of translation into foreign languages are strictly reserved.

ISBN 978-0-573-12081-7

www.samuelfrench-london.co.uk

www.samuelfrench.com

### FOR AMATEUR PRODUCTION ENQUIRIES

#### UNITED KINGDOM AND WORLD EXCLUDING NORTH AMERICA
plays@SamuelFrench-London.co.uk
020 7255 4302/01

Each title is subject to availability from Samuel French,

depending upon country of performance.

CAUTION: Professional and amateur producers are hereby warned that *GROWING PAINS* is subject to a licensing fee. Publication of this play does not imply availability for performance. Both amateurs and professionals considering a production are strongly advised to apply to the appropriate agent before starting rehearsals, advertising, or booking a theatre. A licensing fee must be paid whether the title is presented for charity or gain and whether or not admission is charged.

The professional rights in this play are controlled by Samuel French Ltd, 52 Fitzroy Street, London, W1T 5JR.

No one shall make any changes in this title for the purpose of production. No part of this book may be reproduced, stored in a retrieval system, or transmitted in any form, by any means, now known or yet to be invented, including mechanical, electronic, photocopying, recording, videotaping, or otherwise, without the prior written permission of the publisher. No one shall upload this title, or part of this title, to any social media websites.

The right of Ian Armstrong to be identified as author of this work has been asserted by him in accordance with Section 77 of the Copyright, Designs and Patents Act 1988

# GROWING PAINS

This play was first performed by RAF Halton at the Royal Air Force Theatrical Association's Festival of One-Act Plays held at RAF Stafford in September 1987.

| | |
|---|---|
| **Frank Shaw** | Ian Armstrong |
| **Smith** | John Waldram |
| **Nurse** | Elisabeth Firth |
| **Doctor One** | Chris Coles |
| **Mary Shaw** | Barbara Muston |
| **Miss Jameson** | Jenny Mummery |
| **Mrs Pritchard** | Jenny Mummery |
| **Matron** | Elisabeth Firth |
| **Doctor Two** | Chris Coles |

Directed by Margaret Paton
Lighting by Christine Penman

# CHARACTERS

in order of appearance

**Frank Shaw**
**Smith** (an "expectant father")
**Nurse**
**Doctor One**
**Mary Shaw**
**Miss Jameson** (nursery-school teacher)
**Mr(s) Pritchard** (Head of secondary school)
**Matron**
**Doctor Two**

## Scenes

Scene 1   A Hospital Waiting Room
Scene 2   The Nursery School
Scene 3   The Shaws' House
Scene 4   The Headmaster's Office
Scene 5   The Shaws' House
Scene 6   A Hospital Waiting Room

## PRODUCTION NOTES

Each scene can be enacted on a basically empty stage with the minimum of furniture and props, using imaginative lighting to light acting areas. Scene changes should be carried out quickly and efficiently by the stage-crew during soliloquies and in full view of the audience. The action of the play spans seventeen years in the life of a young boy, Andrew, as seen through the eyes of his parents, Frank and Mary. The other characters can be played by individual actors, or it may be more interesting to "double-up".

# GROWING PAINS

**SCENE 1**

*A Hospital Waiting Room*

*The* CURTAINS *open to reveal the stage in darkness. A telephone rings stridently and a single spot reveals the telephone on a desk situated* DS. *After several rings it stops and the single spot fades. After a pause another spot illuminates Frank who addresses the audience*

**Frank** When Mary first told me she was pregnant I was horrified. I suppose after twelve years of marriage I should have been pleased, and I was later on, but I distinctly remember that my first and most immediate reaction was complete shock. When we first got married we decided to wait a few years until we got established with a home and had some time together. Then the years just slipped by and suddenly—there we were, married for twelve years, having a great time and the envy of all our friends, but for reasons that I can't really explain, empty and, well—bored somehow. I knew Mary had always wanted to be a mum so I eventually let her persuade me to throw caution to the wind. Then, it all seemed to happen so quickly. One minute we were planning a winter holiday and suddenly there we were in Mothercare spending the holiday savings on prams, cots, baby-baths—you name it—we bought it! She bought a whole drawer full of nappies—I'm sure we won't need half of them! The waiting was the difficult bit—I wanted him to come there and then. I've never been the patient type! Finally, when I took Mary into the hospital I thought, "This is it" but it wasn't. I sat there for hours, waiting and waiting . . .

*Full stage lighting comes up to reveal the hospital waiting-room. It is seven forty-five pm. Frank is seated on a chair smoking, and awaiting the birth. He has been waiting round the hospital for some considerable time and is nervous and impatient. Another expectant father, Smith, is also waiting—he sits quietly. Occasionally the two men glance at each other and smile self-consciously. Frank continues to smoke and after a long silence he speaks*

**Frank** Quarter-to-eight. She's been in there for ages.

*A Nurse enters briskly. She crosses the stage, smiles at both men and exits*

Don't say much, do they?
**Smith** Not much—no.

*There is a long silence. Eventually Frank tries to make conversation*

**Frank** You chickened out then?
**Smith** What?
**Frank** Didn't watch.
**Smith** Er—no—I—
**Frank** Yeh—me too!

*There is another long silence. Eventually, Frank crosses to a table, picks up a magazine, returns to his seat and opens the magazine*

*The Doctor enters briskly. He pauses on seeing two men and looks at his file to obtain the name he wants*

*Both men rise in anticipation*

**Doctor** Mr-er-Smith?

*Frank sits*

Good news—your wife's just had a little girl. Six pounds ten ounces—no complications—mother and baby fine.
**Smith** Thank God! (*He sits and then stands up again*) When can I seem them?
**Doctor** She's just on her way back to the ward. Just give nurse a few minutes to tidy up and then you can go in. Nurse will tell you when.
**Smith** Thanks—thanks very much.

*Smith sits down*

*The Doctor looks at Frank, smiles and exits*

**Frank** Typical! He only arrived an hour ago!

*After a pause he looks at Smith who catches him looking*

Congratulations! Baby girl, eh—you pleased?
**Smith** Over the moon! Didn't care about the sex—just so long as
they were both—you know——
**Frank** Yes. Nice size. Six pounds ten ounces—not too big—not
too small—medium.
**Smith** Yes. (*Pause*) What about you, heard anything yet?
**Frank** Not yet. She's been in there for hours.

*The Nurse enters and both men sit up expectantly. She smiles,
picks up something from her desk and exits without speaking*

*The men relax*

Busy, isn't she?
**Smith** What?
**Frank** Smiler (*indicating the nurse*)—always bustling about—
busy.
**Smith** Yes, I hadn't really noticed. Been too worried about—you
know——
**Frank** Yes.

*Silence*

This your first, then?
**Smith** No, we've got three more at home, two boys and a girl.
They're with their grandmother.
**Frank** That's nice—two of each—that's what they call family
planning I suppose.
**Smith** Yes.

*Smith laughs foolishly. Franks laughs too but eventually the laughter
dies and there is silence*

**Frank** This is our first.
**Smith** Really?
**Frank** Yes. We finally decided to start before it's too late. Neither
of us getting any younger. I wanted a boy—someone to carry on
the family name—I'm an only child myself. (*He gets up and
moves impatiently to the exit, turns and moves* DS) I just can't
stand all this waiting around being smiled at like I'm some kind
of idiot or something. I bet she's lying in there fast asleep, while
I'm out here, pacing up and down, worrying myself to death!
**Smith** How old's your wife?

**Frank** Thirty-eight.
**Smith** (*nodding*) I see.

*He continues to nod. Frank looks at him and then looks away*

*The Nurse enters, smiling*

**Nurse** You can go in now, Mr Smith—your wife's ready for you—
second door on the left. (*She sits down behind her desk and starts
to make notes*)
**Smith** Thank you. (*He gets up and picks up an enormous bunch of
flowers from under his chair*) Well—I'll be running along then. I
hope you don't have to wait much longer—I expect everything
will turn out all right. (*He moves towards the exit, then hesitates*)
Yes—well. (*He turns back to Frank*) Bye then?
**Frank** Bye!

*Smith exits*

*Frank watches him go and then begins to pace nervously. As he paces
he realizes the Nurse is watching. He stops. They smile and Frank
sits again. After a pause he looks at his watch, stares at it and then
shakes his wrist and stares again. The Nurse looks up and they smile
again. Frank gets up and selects another magazine—*Woman's
Own*—sits down again and tries to read. He quickly gives up in
despair and drops the magazine on the chair beside him. He rises and
crosses to the nurse*

How's it going?
**Nurse** Oh, fine. It's been very quiet so far tonight. Makes a
pleasant change.
**Frank** No, I meant with my wife—it's been several hours.
**Nurse** Don't worry, Mr Shaw, we're taking very good care of her.
We've just got to be a little careful with a late birth but
everything's fine.
**Frank** You're sure there are no complications?
**Nurse** None at all, Mr Shaw. Just be patient for a bit longer. Take
a stroll around the block—perhaps you'd like a cup of coffee.
**Frank** Coffee sounds good—might help me relax!

*The Doctor strides into the waiting room as the Nurse is rising
from her desk*

**Doctor** Mr Shaw. Congratulations! You're a father—lovely little boy—mother and baby blooming.
**Frank** Ah—ah really? (*He sits*)
**Doctor** Yes, really. He kept us waiting a bit, but he's worth every minute—you'll be able to see him soon—just give us a couple of minutes to clean up. (*He turns to the nurse*) Just a minute, Nurse.

*The Nurse exits with the Doctor*

*Frank sits looking stunned and bewildered and then realizes the full impact*

**Frank** I've done it! I'm a dad! A boy—I knew it would be a boy. (*He rises and moves* DS) I wonder what he looks like? Probably got my nose. I hope he likes fishing! I'll teach him. We can go fishing, watch war films—she won't be able to switch over now there's two of us. It'll be great! I've already bought him a little wind-up train and a Watford bobble-hat. I haven't shown them to Mary yet—she'd only laugh. But I thought, even if it's a girl she could still play trains and lots of girls like football—don't they? We're going to call him Andrew. It's a bit wet but I don't mind really. I can call him Andy—that's OK. Andrew Shaw— sounds OK doesn't it? Not too stuffy—just nice.

*The Nurse enters*

**Nurse** You can go in now, Mr Shaw. Mother and baby are together in the ward. Don't stay too long. Mrs Shaw is bound to be a bit tired.
**Frank** Thank you—it's this way isn't it?

*They both exit*

*The lights dim and Mary enters and moves* DS. *Spot on Mary. At the same time the stage crew enter to strike the hospital scenery and set the school scene. One of the crew provides a chair for Mary*

**Mary** Thank you. (*She sits and addresses the audience*) Eighteen stitches! Eighteen! I'm not sure I wouldn't prefer to stand. Still, it's all been worth it— a dream fulfilled. He was seven pounds three ounces—beautiful little face, blue eyes and lovely black hair. I'm not sure which one of us he looks like—at the moment he's a bit of a wrinkled prune so I suppose he's more like Frank than me. I just can't get over the size of his feet—they're so tiny. I've never seen anything so beautiful. I feel wonderful—really great. Frank's face—he was so funny coming in to see me. He looked completely confused. He'd had a few of course but I didn't mind. I've waited a long time for this moment. I was beginning to think Frank would never give in. It took me eleven years to persuade him that we should start a family. I'm not sure even now if he really wants it. But I kept at him and he agrees with me that we couldn't leave it any longer, and if you don't have kids what's it all about—eh? It seems a bit cold-blooded now but it wasn't at the time. It was quite nice really! The night I conceived, it almost seemed as if we knew what would happen— we took so much care with each other. Never been the same since really, but I don't care—I've got Andrew now and he's absolutely wonderful. He's the most important person in my life—next to Frank, of course. We had a christening for him when he was six weeks old. There weren't many people there— everyone lives so far away—but it was really lovely. A day to remember.

*The spot on Mary fades and she exits*

*A single spot reveals Frank DS*

**Frank** We soon settled back into a routine. I went to work as usual and Mary and Andrew played at home. He was a good baby—well, as good as they can be at that age, I suppose. Mary fed him herself and so after the first night I just slept through. Mind you, I did have to change a few nappies—got quite good at it too—nothing to it if you don't look! I'd never been a baby man before. No experience of kids that age you see. But I loved it—everything. I got a bit worried when he changed to solids— he didn't like it much. He kept throwing up—which was a bit disconcerting when the in-laws came to stay. We tried every- thing—scrambled eggs, fish fingers, chips—but it was no good— all over the table cloth, the high chair—everywhere. He liked crisps though and ice-cream but force him to try cabbage or a brussel sprout and you had to duck pretty fast. But they were happy days. He was a lovely kid and we had some fun.

*The lighting rises a little as Mary enters dressed for her interview with Miss Jameson*

**Mary** Even if it wasn't funny at the time.

**Frank** Like the time he fed laxative to the dog thinking they were doggie chocs.

**Mary** Or the time he fed the budgie with "Flash" thinking it was bird-seed.

**Frank** It was a clean death!

**Mary** We used to play together for hours and I used to read to him.

**Frank** She was always buying him books—our attic is lined in cardboard boxes filled with children's books.

**Mary** I'm saving them for my grand-children! Besides it was worth it—he was quite a good little reader by the time he went to nursery school.

**Frank** When he went to nursery school I felt a bit sad—for Mary mainly. Those early years are really special and they are over too quickly.

**Mary** I didn't mind. He was growing up. It was his first, big step into the world outside.

**Frank** Still, it meant Mary had a few hours to herself each day and she enjoyed that.

**Mary** But I worried. I worried about how he was behaving, worried about how he got on with other kids.

*Mary turns* US

**Frank** I told her she'd nothing to worry about—if there had been anything wrong the teacher would have told her.

*Frank exits*

*The lights come up to reveal Mary talking to Miss Jameson, the nursery-school teacher*

Scene 2

*The Nursery School*

**Mary** What seems to be the problem, Miss Jameson? Has Andrew been fighting with the other children? I'm so sorry, it's because he's an only child you see—he's always been on his own—

always used to getting his own way—not having to share things—you know.

**Miss Jameson** It's not that, Mrs Shaw. It's nothing like that. I'm a little concerned with Andrew's reading—I just wanted to ask what he reads when he's at home.

**Mary** Reads?

**Miss Jameson** Yes. Does he read at home? I know he's only four but does he have access to story books and things like that?

**Mary** Well, of course. He has lots of story books—we're always buying them for him. I read to him all the time—he won't go to sleep without a story.

**Miss Jameson** You read to him?

**Mary** Yes—every night.

**Miss Jameson** Does he read to you?

**Mary** Yes, sometimes. He's been reading for over a year now. Basic books, nothing very difficult. He prefers me to read to him though. Is anything wrong? I mean—is there something we don't know.

**Miss Jameson** Well—I've started the children on a new story-book, "Amanda and her Furry Friends". All the children take turns at reading it out loud. They really enjoy it. Except Andrew. He doesn't seem to want to read. I thought perhaps he
, couldn't read but then I remembered you telling me on his first day at school that he could.

**Mary** He reads to me all the time—nearly every night.

**Miss Jameson** Well, he won't read for me. He just stares at the book and says nothing.

**Mary** I can't understand.

**Miss Jameson** Tell me, have you ever had his eyes tested, Mrs Shaw?

**Mary** No—why do you think there's a problem?

**Miss Jameson** I'm not saying there's a problem, Mrs Shaw. I just think it might be worthwhile having him tested. There must be some reason he won't read for me and we wouldn't want him to fall behind would we? So, if he needs glasses or is a little dyslexic then we need to ...

**Mary** Dyslexic!

**Miss Jameson** Oh, I'm sure he's not, Mrs Shaw but we need to find out, don't we? We need to find out what's preventing him from reading.

**Mary** I'll make an appointment straight away. I wasn't expecting anything like this, I mean, you don't, do you? It's always someone else's child isn't it? I'll get him checked at once.

*Mary stands as if to leave*

**Miss Jameson** (*standing-up quickly*) There was just one more thing, Mrs Shaw. I thought I ought to mention it before one of the other mothers told you. I'm not very pleased with Andrew's behaviour in the toilets.

**Mary** I beg your pardon?

**Miss Jameson** Andrew does naughty things in the toilets. The other children think it's very amusing. I'm sure if their mothers knew they wouldn't be quite so pleased.

**Mary** What is it, Miss Jameson? What does he do?

**Miss Jameson** It's more what he doesn't do, I'm afraid. He doesn't use the toilet—he just uses the wall.

**Mary** The wall!

**Miss Jameson** Yes. We only have one toilet and all the children have to use it, plus myself of course, and we don't allow anyone to close the door in case they lock themselves in. When it's Andrew's turn and he sees the others watching—he does it against the wall. They all think it's very funny of course and the more they laugh the more he does it. Now, he does it all the time! I've tried scolding him but without any success, I'm afraid. I was just wondering if you'd experienced this problem at home.

**Mary** No! He's always been very good—we've never had anything like this. I'm ever so sorry, Miss Jameson. I just don't understand what he can be thinking of.

**Miss Jameson** Well, perhaps you'd like to speak to Andrew, Mrs Shaw. We do expect four-year-olds to be properly toilet trained—we just couldn't cope if they all behaved in that way. I'm afraid, if he doesn't improve, Mrs Shaw, we won't be able to let him come any more.

**Mary** Oh, I will, Miss Jameson—I'll give him a good talking to. It won't happen again, I assure you.

*The lights fade to a single spot on Mary, who sits with her head bowed. Slowly, she looks up and addresses the audience. As she speaks the stage is reset for the next scene*

How awful! How embarrassing! To have to sit there and listen to stories of your child peeing up the wall! He probably tries to pee a little higher every day! They'll be having competitions soon to see who can pee the highest. Men! Just because it sticks out in front on some kind of universal joint they think it's for waving with! I couldn't wait to get him home—gave him a right talking to I can tell you. He didn't say anything, he just stared at my feet and after I'd ranted and raved at him for about ten minutes he just looked up, a big tear running down his cheek, and he said, "Sorry Mummy". It didn't work, of course—I had to be hard—I made him promise never to do it again. Then I put him to bed—I was determined to punish him. It didn't last long. The other kids were building a snowman and he looked so sad at the window holding his face in his hands that I snuggled him up in his coat and scarf and sent him outside to play. I was just thinking about his reading problems when Frank came home early.

*Mary picks up some sewing and the Lights come up to reveal the Shaws' lounge/dining room*


SCENE 3


*The Shaws' house*

**Frank** (*off*) Mary!
**Mary** In here.

   *Frank enters*

You're home early—it's just gone three.
**Frank** Mary, I've just seen Andrew playing in the snow.
**Mary** Yes, dear.
**Frank** But he's wearing pink wellingtons.
**Mary** Yes, dear.
**Frank** Who's he pinched them from?
**Mary** They're his, don't you remember? Auntie Maggie gave them to us when Sarah grew out of them.
**Frank** But he's a boy!
**Mary** They're perfectly good wellingtons, Frank, they've hardly been used.

**Frank**  Boys don't wear pink wellingtons!

**Mary**  Four-year-old boys can wear any colour they like Frank—nobody minds what a four-year-old wears.

**Frank**  Well, I mind. I'm not having my son running around outside in pink wellingtons.

**Mary**  Well, you'll have to buy him some new ones then. I'm not letting him out in this weather without something on his feet.

**Frank**  If you had told me he didn't have any I could have bought some weeks ago. Why didn't you tell me?

**Mary**  But he did have some, darling. I just didn't realize that the colour would determine the sexual preferences of a four-year-old, that's all.

**Frank**  I'm not saying it does, Mary, but I just don't want it for my kid. I don't want the other kids poking fun at him.

**Mary**  Nobody's poking fun at him, Frank. I doubt if the other kids are aware of them. Andrew loves them.

**Frank**  Yes—well we'll get him a new pair on Saturday.

**Mary**  It's all right if he plays in them until then, is it? I mean, it's not going to be too late by then, is it? "Parents drive four-year-old into sexual depravity."

**Frank**  Don't be a smart-ass. What's for tea?

**Mary**  Well, I bought some liver as a special treat but I'm not sure you deserve it now.

**Frank**  I haven't had liver in weeks!

**Mary**  Anyway, I haven't started it yet, I didn't expect you this early. Do you want it now?

**Frank**  No, I'll just have a cup of tea now and dinner at the usual time, but I must have a pee first. (*He turns as if to exit*)

**Mary**  Mind the wall!

**Frank**  (*turning back to Mary*) What?

**Mary**  Nothing. I'll put the kettle on.

**Frank**  Fine.


*He turns again to go but just as he is about to exit*


**Mary**  I went to the school today.

**Frank**  School?

**Mary**  Andrew's school—his nursery school. It's my week. Miss Jameson asked me to pop in when I dropped the kids off.

**Frank**  What did she want?

**Mary** She's worried about Andrew. She thinks he's a bad influence on the other children.

**Frank** Bad influence? You mean he's been dishing out my fags again, or trying to convert them to militant tendency—something like that.

**Mary** No!

**Frank** I'll bet he's been trying to make them all wear pink!

**Mary** It's serious, Frank. When it's his turn to read out loud he just sits there and won't say anything. Miss Jameson is very worried, she's tried everything but he just sits there. She's worried about the effect on the other children. If he won't read they might do the same.

**Frank** Well, we know he can read—he's been reading since he was three. Perhaps he just doesn't like the story.

**Mary** It's only a first primer, he should be able to manage those.

**Frank** What's it called?

**Mary** "Amanda and her Furry Friends".

**Frank** Well, there you are, that's your answer.

**Mary** What?

**Frank** Would you want to read "Amanda and her Furry Friends"? Tell her to try him on Harold Robbins.

**Mary** You're a big help. This could be very serious, Frank. Miss
· Jameson thinks he may be dyslexic or something—she thinks we ought to have him tested.

**Frank** Look, Mary. He reads to us doesn't he? I mean, when we put him to bed first he reads, then we read, isn't that right?

**Mary** Yes.

**Frank** So how can he be dyslexic? He reads when he wants to. Tell Miss Jameson she's talking crap!

**Mary** She knows what she's talking about, Frank; she's an experienced nursery teacher. She thinks he's falling behind the other children.

**Frank** For Christ's sake, Mary—you said it yourself—he's only four. How can he be falling behind? Life isn't competitive at four! Some kids can't read at all at that age.

**Mary** I'm just telling you what she thinks.

**Frank** Well she's talking rubbish! Is that it then? Can I have my pee now?

**Mary** (*uncertainly*) Yes, that's it.

**Frank** What's that look for? Was there something else?

**Mary** (*chickening out*) No, that's all it was. Go and sort yourself out. I'll get your tea.

*Frank exits*

*Mary watches him go and then moves* DS

We never did find out why he wouldn't read in class. I had his eyes tested but there was nothing worng. A couple of weeks later you couldn't stop him. He read all the time in school and got very shirty if Miss Jameson asked anyone else to read. Strange, isn't it? Frank's probably right—he just didn't like the story book. But it made me think. There was a little independent mind at work inside him that I wasn't aware of. I was surprised and just a little bit scared. He's a little person all on his own—it's frightening really. I never told Frank about the toilet incident. I worried about it though—I still do sometimes. Isn't it silly? For weeks afterwards I kept going into the bathroom after he'd been—just to check—just to make sure.

*Frank enters* DS

**Frank** The next big event was Andrew's first day at proper school.
**Mary** At primary school. He didn't have to wear a blazer or anything but we bought him a school jumper and tie and a little brown satchel.
**Frank** I bought him an Incredible Hulk lunch-box!
**Mary** We were so proud of him.

*They both break* US. *Frank sits at the dining table smoking a pipe and reading a newspaper while Mary bustles about setting the table for tea*

We began a new phase in our lives. For the first time in years I had some time during the day all to myself. I was kept pretty busy around the house of course, but I had time to go shopping with my friend Shirley. We could afford to take our time—we didn't have the kids tugging at our skirts. It was nice just to go for coffee without having the kids around. But I missed him and I was surprised at how lonely I felt without him.

*Mary continues to set the table. Frank lowers his paper and speaks*

**Frank** I got promoted at work to sales manager with five salesmen

working for me in different areas. It meant I had to spend a lot
of time away from home and sometimes I didn't see Andrew for
days. I'd phone him of course—but it wasn't the same. I missed
him a lot.

**Mary** Didn't you miss me then?

**Frank** Well, of course I did. You can cope without me though—
and, anyway, I was always home at weekends.

**Mary** Weekends were lovely. I'd make us all breakfast and bring
it upstairs on a tray and we'd all three have breakfast in the
same bed. Andrew in the middle—I loved that! (*There is a pause
while she continues setting the table then she stops and speaks*) I
can't remember when I first suspected Frank of seeing another
woman. There were signs, I suppose, but they didn't register at
first. We didn't make love very often, we just didn't seem to need
to or want to. It tailed off after Andrew was born. It didn't
worry me—at first. I hadn't really wanted to—just now and
again when I was nervous or frightened. There was no lipstick
on collars or anything like that. Just a lot of tiny incidents that
seemed to creep up on me and then, suddenly, I knew! Everything fell into place. (*She turns and sits at the table*)

**Frank** Rachel Smith! Unmarried, twenty-six years old, knew what
she wanted and didn't muck about. She was a buyer for a firm
up north. She kept my order book full, I can tell you! At first it
was just a bit of fun—I don't think either of us took it very
seriously. She was young and I was flattered and—well—I've
also been curious about—other women—you know. But it was
just a fling! Then, after I'd been seeing her for about a year, I
began to get very nervous. I took a lot of care to make sure
Mary never found out. God, if she'd ever suspected that I was
having an affair it would have been catastrophic—didn't bear
thinking about. (*He goes back to reading his paper*)

**Mary** Who is it, then?

*There is a pregnant silence. Then, without lowering the paper, Frank
responds*

**Frank** Who is what?

**Mary** I'm not stupid Frank, I know you're seeing someone—who
is it?

*Frank lowers the paper and stares at her for a long time. He is trying
to decide whether to bluff it out or not—he doesn't*

**Frank** She works for a customer up north.
**Mary** You bastard! (*Her head drops and there is a pause before she continues*) What's her name?
**Frank** Does it matter?
**Mary** I want to know!
**Frank** Rachel.
**Mary** Rachel what?
**Frank** Rachel! It doesn't matter about her surname.
**Mary** How old is she?
**Frank** Twenty-six.
**Mary** Is she married?
**Frank** No.
**Mary** Why, Frank? Why?
**Frank** I don't know—it just happened. I didn't mean it to go on this long.
**Mary** How often do you see her?
**Frank** Not often—every six weeks, something like that.
**Mary** Do you love her?
**Frank** I don't think so.
**Mary** What does that mean?
**Frank** I don't know! I like her—I like being with her—I just don't know.
**Mary** And me—how do you feel about me?
**Frank** I love you—you know I do.
**Mary** Do I?
**Frank** Yes!
**Mary** You love us both then—is that it?
**Frank** I suppose I do in a way—but it's different.
**Mary** You mean with her it's fun—the sex.
**Frank** That's part of it.
**Mary** So I'm to blame, am I? For not wanting to make love.
**Frank** I'm not blaming you—it's not your fault—it's just the way we are. You don't seem to want me or need me—physically— you can't help that—you don't need that side of things very often. I'm not like that. I need a physical relationship but I don't want to have to demand it from you. Perhaps we should have talked about it.
**Mary** So, what happens now? Are you going to leave me for her? Does she want you to leave me?
**Frank** Yes.

**Mary**  Bitch! What did you say?
**Frank**  I told her I couldn't—that I wouldn't——
**Mary**  And what did she say?
**Frank**  She hopes I'll change my mind.
**Mary**  And will you?
**Frank**  I'd never leave you, Mary—not if you want me to stay.
**Mary**  Well, you can't have both of us. You've got to choose one way or the other. It may suit your purpose to have me sitting at home looking after your son while you jump in and out of bed with her but I want no part of it. What are you going to do about it?
**Frank**  What do you want me to do? Do you want me to go?
**Mary**  At first I did. I'm not sure any more. I hated you! I couldn't understand how you could hurt us this way. But I've had time to think about it. I can't forgive you, Frank—you've hurt me, you've hurt us both, but I won't hurt Andrew. He loves you—he needs you—he wouldn't understand.
**Frank**  I'll phone her. I'll phone her tomorrow and tell her it's all over.
**Mary**  Doesn't she even deserve a visit or a letter?
**Frank**  It's better like this.
**Mary**  Will she be upset?
**Frank**  I expect so, yes.
**Mary**  Good!

*Mary turns away and exits*

*Frank rises and calls after her*

**Frank**  I'm sorry.

*His head drops and, after a pause, he turns away* DS. *The lights fade to a single spot on Frank and during the next speech the stage is set for the Headmaster's office. Frank becomes aware of the presence of the audience, and although he feels slightly embarrassed, he addresses them*

That was it! I'd worried myself sick for months about her finding out and that was it! Things were a bit strained after that—though not as bad as I expected. We even continued sleeping in the same bed—I wasn't banished to the spare room or anything like that. But sex was out! I knew better than to try, of course, so I wasn't actually refused. Otherwise, everything appeared reasonably normal on the surface. She obviously planned it that way for Andrew's sake. I spoke to Rachel the next day and broke the news. I haven't seen her or heard from her since. She left the company soon after and so, that was that—memories.

*Mary enters with Frank's raincoat and crosses into the acting area*

(*Putting on his raincoat*) The years passed and eventually Andrew went to secondary modern

**Mary** He did well, too—always got good results in his term exams.

**Frank** Except English! He wasn't into Shakespeare, Dickens or stuff like that. More of a "Hawaii Five-O" man—if you know what I mean.

**Mary** Then, out of the blue, we were summoned to see the Headmaster.

*The lights come up fully to reveal the Headmaster's office. The Head is seated behind his desk and as Frank and Mary cross to meet him, he stands up*

SCENE 4

*The Headmaster's Office*

**Head** Good morning, Mr and Mrs Shaw—do sit down. Isn't it a dreadful morning, so much for a bright sunny day with the odd shower.

**Mary** Dreadful, isn't it?

**Frank** You wanted to see us, Headmaster.

**Head** Yes, Mr Shaw. I thought it best.

**Mary** What's happened—is it serious? It's about Andrew isn't it?

**Head** I'm afraid so—you see on Monday we caught Andrew and some other pupils illegally absent from school. They'd skipped classes and gone to a local cinema.

**Frank** Doesn't sound too serious to me!

**Head** (*ignoring Frank's comment*) We were very surprised. Andrew's normally very well behaved.

**Mary**  It's not like him, Mr Pritchard, he enjoys school—well, he seems to.

**Head**  It's not the first time this has happened, I'm afraid, so when Mr Farmer complained that five of his English Lit. class were missing we decided to investigate. I had my suspicions that it involved the local cinema and so I asked the manager to watch out for them. He phoned me as soon as they had checked in.

**Frank**  Cunning bastard!

**Head**  I beg your pardon?

**Frank**  He phoned after they had bought a ticket.

**Head**  That's hardly the point, Mr Shaw. I was grateful for his help. I went to the cinema myself and brought them back to school.

**Mary**  Andrew hasn't mentioned this to us. He must have known we'd find out.

**Head**  I have been keeping them a little in suspense, Mrs Shaw. Not deliberately, of course, but I needed time to discuss the matter with the School Governors.

**Frank**  Does it need to go that far, Mr Pritchard—I mean surely this is something best handled between us.

**Head**  It's not quite that simple. We have a duty to other parents to maintain the reputation of the school and that includes ensuring that the school's regulations are not flouted. We can't allow the example set by these students to go unpunished. I'm not allowed to cane them or anything like that but I need to obtain approval for an equitable punishment for them all—the boys and the girls.

**Mary**  Girls!

**Frank**  There were girls as well?

**Head**  There were two girls and three boys—and I regret to inform you that the Governors and I have decided that all those involved must be sent home for one week.

**Frank**  Sent home—what sort of punishment is that? He'll think it's a holiday.

**Head**  We'll give them plenty of work to do, Mr Shaw, and ultimately we rely on your support to ensure that the time spent at home is not regarded as a holiday. There was some mention of banning them altogether or at least until the end of term but I managed to persuade the Governors that a week was sufficient.

**Mary**  We are grateful, Mr Pritchard. A week at home cooling his heels will bring him to his senses, I'm sure, and you can rely on Frank and me to ensure that he works hard. Can't he, Frank?

**Frank** Yes, of course.

**Head** There was one other point I must just mention. Two of the boys and one of the girls were smoking when I found them. Andrew was one of the smokers.

**Frank** Bloody little fool!

**Head** It seems that Andrews was the only one to purchase cigarettes. They were all smoking cigarettes supplied by Andrew. The school rules are quite specific about smoking. We don't allow them to smoke in school and smoking outside in uniform is also a very serious breach of school discipline.

**Frank** (*to Mary*) I told you he got too much pocket-money!

**Mary** He gets the same as most kids his age, Frank; he certainly doesn't get much more.

**Head** Well perhaps that's something you can discuss at home, Mr and Mrs Shaw. As far as the school is concerned, we feel strongly that this additional crime shouldn't go unpunished and since Andrew was the instigator, the supplier, as it were, I'm afraid he must suffer an additional week at home.

**Mary** Two weeks!

**Frank** What about the others? They smoked too!

**Head** We've discussed it fully, Mr Shaw—two weeks for Andrew and one week for the rest. I think under the circumstances he's getting off very lightly.

**Frank** Well, I'm not sure that I agree.

*Mary looks at him anxiously*

... but I'll accept your decision, of course, in this case.

**Head** I'm glad you see it that way. Andrew is a good pupil. He doesn't normally give us any trouble and Lord knows we have plenty who do. I shall see them later today and tell them the punishment and of course they'll get a good dressing down at the same time. I hope I can rely on your support to ensure that this punishment is not treated as time-off and to remind Andrew of the standards we all expect from him.

**Frank** Yes of course. He'll get a bloody good talking to when he gets home.

**Head** Well then, I don't think I need detain you any longer. Nice to have seen you both of course, but I wish it had been under happier circumstances.

*They all stand*

**Mary** So do we, Mr Pritchard—thank you for letting us know. You've been very kind.
**Frank** Yes—thank you, Mr Pritchard—sorry you've been put to all this trouble.

*Frank and Mary move* DS. *The lights change to allow the set to be struck*

SCENE 5

*The Shaws' House*

**Mary** Hypocrite!
**Frank** What?
**Mary** You—telling him off for bunking off school and smoking. Your mother told me you were always bunking off sports afternoons and you told me yourself you've been smoking since
· you were fourteen.
**Frank** Just because I did, it doesn't make it right, does it? He's supposed to learn from our mistakes and not make the same ones all over again, isn't he?
**Mary** He's got a long way to go before he makes all the mistakes you made, hasn't he?
**Frank** Very funny—you're supposed to be on my side. I mean we did promise to give him a good talking to.
**Mary** Where is he now?
**Frank** Upstairs.
**Mary** Is he upset?
**Frank** Of course he's upset—he's more than upset—he's bloody furious that he got found out! Now if you mean remorseful or regretful—no, I don't think he is. Not a bit!
**Mary** Oh dear—I'd better go and talk to him.
**Frank** Oh no! I've just given him a right bollocking—I don't want you going all soft with him.
**Mary** Well, he can't stay up there all night—it's nearly tea-time.

**Frank** I doubt if he wants any—not if he has to come down. Just leave him for a while. If he hasn't come down by the time it's ready then you can take it up—but don't go near him just yet.

**Mary** (*smiling*) He's a little devil isn't he? Skiving off school, smoking in the cinema, girls. Whatever next?

**Frank** It's not supposed to be amusing, you know. How can he know it's wrong if you sit there giggling about it. If we don't stop him now who knows what he'll try next.

**Mary** (*after she has stopped giggling*) Do you think he's a virgin, Frank.

**Frank** Who?

**Mary** Andrew. He's fifteen now and talking to girls in the cinema and smoking.

**Frank** Not very likely then, is it? Fifteen and talking to girls—he's probably had half the fourth form by now.

**Mary** Oh—be serious. I mean, it's possible he isn't—how would we know?

**Frank** (*laughing*) You can't tell can you? Not unless his hair drops out! He's fifteen. Boys know a lot at fifteen, or think they do. He's bound to experiment, to try it on.

**Mary** Did you experiment when you were fifteen?

**Frank** Of course—boys do—and girls too, since boys have to experiment with someone.

**Mary** I didn't. I don't even remember being groped before I met you. It's different now, I suppose. Kids seem to know much more than I ever did. I think that's a bit sad.

**Frank** I don't think you need to worry about Andrew. If he was really into girls and sex—we'd know about it.

**Mary** Like we knew about him smoking!

**Frank** He's a virgin—trust me—I'd know if he wasn't. We talk when we're fishing—men's stuff. Things he wouldn't dream of talking to you about. If he wasn't a virgin I'd know about it.

**Mary** I hope so. He's too young! I don't want him to get into all that too soon. It's funny isn't it? I want him to be a man, a husband, a father, but in a way I'll be sad when it happens. I enjoy his innocence—I'll regret it when it's gone. Sometimes it can be painful growing up—I just want to keep him from being hurt.

**Frank** You can't keep him from being hurt, that's all part of growing up, isn't it? The pains! Most of us go through it and turn out OK. You can't protect him—I'm not sure you even ought to try. Life isn't any less painful when you're older—you may not be doing him a favour.

**Mary** Oh—I know—but I can't help it. I don't want him to grow up too soon. I'm not ready yet.

*Pause*

**Frank** Has he told you he wants a motorbike?
**Mary** Yes.
**Frank** What do you think about it?
**Mary** I'm not happy, Frank, I'm not happy at all. I hate them. They're noisy and dangerous. You read about so many horrific accidents and it's always a young boy on a motorbike. I don't want him to have one, Frank—I'd lie awake every night worrying about it.
**Frank** It won't be that bad. He's a sensible boy; he's not a young hothead. I'm sure he'll be careful.

*Pause*

**Mary** You're with him on this—you're taking his side.
**Frank** I'm not taking sides. He'll be sixteen soon. All his chums have bikes—he rides pillion all the time. I don't see the difference. At least if he was driving he'd be in charge and could take care. As it is he has no control at all.
**Mary** I don't care. I don't even like him riding pillion and I've told him not to. I asked you to speak to him but you won't. You think I'm wrong, don't you.
**Frank** Mary, all teenage boys dream about owning a motorbike. It's natural.
**Mary** You've already agreed, haven't you? You've already told him he can have one.
**Frank** No, I just promised I'd talk with you.
**Mary** But he knows you're all for it, doesn't he?
**Frank** I've always liked bikes, he knows that. He knows I used to own one myself at his age—we've never made any secret of that.
**Mary** Don't you worry? Aren't you scared about what could happen? He's your son—why aren't you frightened of what might happen?
**Frank** I do worry, but I can't be frightened about what might happen. You can't wrap him up in cotton wool. Sooner or later

he'll do what he wants whether we approve or not. If he doesn't get a bike now he'll get one when he's eighteen. If we let him have it now perhaps he'll respect our approval and ride it sensibly so as not to scare us.

**Mary** Well, on your own head be it then. But he's not having it yet. Not while he's in disgrace over this school business. I'm not having him sent home from school and then giving him a motorbike as some kind of reward.

**Frank** When can he have it then?

**Mary** If he has to have it—it had better be for his birthday but you'd both better start saving—you needn't expect any help from me.

**Frank** I'll tell him—he'll be over the moon.

*Frank exits*

*The lights fade to a single spot on Mary. As she talks the set is changed to the hospital waiting-room*

**Mary** Was I wrong? Is a mother ever wrong when she fears for her child's safety. Thousands of kids have motorbikes so thousands of mothers can't feel like I do. Am I so different? I didn't feel wrong and I didn't understand why Frank didn't feel as I did. I just couldn't go on being always the one to say no. They bought the bike on Andrew's birthday. It was quite a nice motorbike really—50cc—whatever that means. In no time at all he passed his test then he went everywhere on it. He still went fishing and the bike allowed him to go further afield. In the end, even I stopped worrying.

*Mary pauses, moves* us *and sits. The telephone rings and a spot picks out the phone on the nurse's desk. After three rings the ringing stops, the spot fades and Mary resumes*

I was at home when the police called. They didn't say how it happened or what state he was in—just that he was badly hurt and that I must get to the hospital immediately. I just broke down—couldn't stop crying. The police rang Frank at work and told him to meet us at the hospital. They sent a car for me—I don't remember much about the journey—and when I got there Frank was waiting. We waited and waited. Everyone was rushing about but no one spoke to us. We just sat in silence, each of us thinking our own thoughts.

*The lights come up to reveal the hospital waiting-room*


SCENE 6

*A Hospital Waiting-room*

*Frank and Mary are sitting—Mary stares into space, Frank has his elbows on his knees supporting his face. After a pause Frank speaks*

**Frank** What time is it?
**Mary** Twenty-five to.
**Frank** Why doesn't someone tell us what's happening?
**Mary** Be patient, they're doing what they can.

*There is silence*

**Frank** That bike—that bloody bike! Why didn't I listen to you? If I hadn't said he could have that bike he wouldn't be here.
**Mary** Please Frank, not now.
**Frank** I should have listened to you.
**Mary** It's what he wanted, Frank, we've always tried to give him whatever he wanted.
**Frank** Well that's where we failed then. We should have been stronger—I should have been stronger.
**Mary** It's in the past—we can't change it.
**Frank** Well, he won't ride that bike again, I can change that. I'll get rid of it tomorrow.
**Mary** The police say it's a write-off—completely smashed.

*Frank stares at her and then looks away. After a pause Frank gets up and moves away* DS

*Matron enters*

**Matron** Mr and Mrs Shaw? The doctor's on his way—he's just washing-up. Can I get you anything—a cup of tea?
**Mary** No, thank you.
**Matron** You're sure?
**Mary** Please, how is our son? It's been nearly two hours.

**Matron** The doctor's just coming, Mrs Shaw.

*The Matron exits*

*Frank and Mary exchange glances. Mary is close to tears. She looks away and Frank crosses to her, puts his arm around her and sits*

*The door opens and the Doctor enters*

*Frank and Mary immediately stand up*

**Doctor** Mr and Mrs Shaw?
**Mary** How is he Doctor? How is our son?
**Frank** We've been here nearly two hours. Nobody's told us what's going on.
**Doctor** Yes, I'm very sorry, Mr Shaw, but we've been kept very busy.
**Frank** Well, surely someone could have spoken to us.
**Doctor** It was an extremely nasty accident, Mr Shaw—motor-cycle accidents usually are—we've tried just about everything to save him but I'm afraid ...
**Frank** What? What are you trying to tell us?
**Doctor** Please ... sit down, sit down, Mrs Shaw.

*They all sit down*

I'm afraid we have to be prepared for the worst.
**Mary** Oh no. (*She bursts into tears*)
**Frank** Worst?
**Doctor** I'm afraid so. Technically your son is dead. I'm sorry.
**Frank** Technically? I don't understand.
**Doctor** It's difficult to explain, Mr Shaw, but, yes, as far as medical opinion is concerned, Andrew is dead. We've got him on a life support machine and his heart is still beating but there is no EEG response. Without support, I'm afraid, he would ...
**Mary** I don't understand—his heart is still beating?
**Frank** He means that the machine is keeping him alive.
**Doctor** Yes, that's it. It was a terrible smash and we did everything we could to save him, but it was hopeless—technically he was dead on arrival.
**Mary** But if he's breathing there must be some hope—isn't there?
**Doctor** He's not actually breathing, Mrs Shaw. We are keeping his

heart beating and his lungs going by artificial means but if we stopped the machine then everything would stop.

**Frank** Can't we keep it going?

**Doctor** It would serve no purpose, I'm afraid. Andrew won't recover. We need to be able to switch off.

**Mary** No!

**Frank** Switch off! (*Then it hits him*) Just a minute! Are you saying it's our decision?

**Doctor** I'd like your consent.

**Mary** But that's not for us to decide—surely you decide? We're his parents; we can't make a decision like that.

**Frank** You're asking us to kill our son! Do you really need our permission.

**Doctor** No, Mr Shaw, I don't need your permission—but I would prefer to have your consent.

**Frank** (*furious*) How can you expect us to say, "Switch off". We're his parents, for God's sake. We want you to save him.

**Doctor** I know exactly how you feel, Mr Shaw. It's difficult, I know, but technically Andrew is already dead—his brain is dead.

**Frank** Damn it! You didn't have to tell us. You could have just switched off and told us he was dead. We wouldn't have known.

**Doctor** I'm sorry, I can't do that. I would like your consent.

**Frank** Why? Why do you need to involve us? Can't you accept the responsibility—is that it?

**Mary** Frank, please . . .

**Frank** Well, I've got news for you, Doctor. If you think we're going to relieve you of this, you're wrong, quite wrong. We won't kill our son!

**Mary** Frank don't . . . Doctor, we need to talk about this, we need time.

**Doctor** Of course, Mrs Shaw, there's plenty of time. Please—talk it over. I'll be in the ward, just call if you need me.

*The Doctor exits*

*There is silence. Franks sits down and slowly Mary joins him. After a pause she puts her arm around him and speaks*

**Mary** Frank . . . talk to me.

**Frank** Bloody doctors—all those years of training and when

they're on the spot, when they're forced to make a big de-
cision—they're shit scared—just like you and me.
**Mary** He can't help it, Frank. It's not his fault.
**Frank** I can't do it, love. He's our son.
**Mary** I know, Frank.
**Frank** He only lived seventeen years and it's all been totally
useless. After we waited so long, why did God give us a child
that was going to die before he had a chance to live?
**Mary** I don't know ... I don't know. It's like a dream. I can't
believe it's happening to us—it all seems so unreal. What time is
it?
**Frank** Quarter to ten.
**Mary** He wasn't due home for over an hour yet. You told him to
be in by eleven. I keep thinking if we go home it will be all right.
He'll just come in at eleven o'clock and everything will be OK.
**Frank** Do you want to go home? We don't need to decide
anything tonight.
**Mary** There's no point. We can't put it off Frank—I don't want
him in some kind of limbo. We have to help him Frank—one
last time. We have to give him peace. Don't you see?
**Frank** (*after a pause*) I do see—I see it all very clearly—and I feel
empty inside. He was all that I lived for, Mary. Without
Andrew, what's left?
**Mary** How strange thoughts are at a time like this. Do you
remember the night we made him Frank?
**Frank** It was long ago.
**Mary** It was a whole life time ago. There weren't any complica-
tions then. It was special—we cared for each other then.
**Frank** It was different then—a lot has happened in seventeen
years.
**Mary** Was it, Frank? Was it really so different?
**Frank** Don't confuse me!
**Mary** Think about it, Frank. Think about Andrew—how we
loved him—how he loved us—how we loved each other.
**Frank** I remember a little fair-haired boy—running up the garden,
laughing and giggling and jumping into my arms shouting,
"Save me, Daddy, save me!"
**Mary** He loved you, Frank ... we both did.
**Frank** It all seems to have passed so quickly. His first day at
school, then secondary school, confirmation and then he was

nearly a man. He thought we didn't know he smoked and you wondered if he thought about sex.

**Mary** I asked him, you know—I asked him if he'd ever been with a girl. He wouldn't give me a straight answer but he hadn't, I could tell. I could see it in his eyes. It seems so silly now.

**Frank** He won't do any of it now. We've lost him, love.

**Mary** We haven't lost him Frank. We'll never lose him, he'll always be there. He won't change or get any older and he won't be hurt anymore. We can still love him. No matter how long we live or what happens to us we'll always have him and each other. Nothing can hurt us. Even if we lose each other it won't be for long and then we'll all be together again—just the three of us— forever.

**Frank** And to hell with the rest of them, love—to hell with them.

**Mary** So, we have to decide, Frank. What are we going to do?

**Frank** (*after a long pause*) We're going to help him love—we're going to help him one last time. (*He takes her hands*) Now, dry those tears—that's it—and give me a big hug.

*They hug*

**Mary** Oh Frank!

**Frank** Now hold my hand, Mary—and let's go and find our son.

*They exit slowly as the lights fade to Black-out*

# FURNITURE AND PROPERTY LIST

## Scene 1

*On stage:* **Desk.** *On it:* telephone, papers, pen. *Behind it:* chair
2 chairs. *Under one chair:* bunch of flowers
Low table. *On it:* magazines

*Personal:* **Frank:** cigarettes, lighter, watch
**Doctor One:** file

## Scene 2

*On stage:* 2 chairs

## Scene 3

*On stage:* Dining table. *On it:* crockery, cutlery
2 dining chairs

*Off stage:* Raincoat (**Mary**)

*Personal:* **Mary:** sewing
**Frank:** pipe, newspaper

## Scene 4

*On stage:* Desk. *Behind it:* chair
2 chairs

## Scene 5

*On stage:* Living-room furniture

## Scene 6

*On stage:* Desk. *On it:* telephone, papers. *Behind it:* chair
2 chairs
Low table. *On it:* magazines

# LIGHTING PLOT

*To open:*  *Black-out*

| | | |
|---|---|---|
| *Cue* 1 | Telephone rings<br>*Spot on telephone* | (Page 1) |

*Cue* 1  Telephone rings         (Page 1)
*Spot on telephone*

*Cue* 2  Telephone stops ringing.         (Page 1)
*Fade spot on telephone. Pause. Spot up on front*

*Cue* 3  **Frank:** "... waiting and waiting ..."         (Page 1)
*Full stage lighting*

*Cue* 4  **Frank** and **Nurse** exit         (Page 5)
*Fade lights. Spot on Mary*

*Cue* 5  **Mary:** "A day to remember."         (Page 6)
*Cut spot on Mary. Spot on Frank* DS

*Cue* 6  **Frank:** "... we had some fun."         (Page 6)
*Increase lighting*

*Cue* 7  **Frank:** "... teacher would have told her."         (Page 7)
*Full stage lighting for Scene 2*

*Cue* 8  **Mary:** "I assure you."         (Page 9)
*Fade light to a single spot on Mary*

*Cue* 9  **Mary** picks up some sewing         (Page 10)
*Full stage lighting for Scene 3*

*Cue* 10  **Frank:** "I'm sorry."         (Page 16)
*Fade light to a single spot on Frank*

*Cue* 11  **Mary:** "... summoned to see the Headmaster."         (Page 17)
*Full stage lighting for Scene 4*

*Cue* 12  **Frank:** "... all this trouble."         (Page 20)
*Fade light for scene change then up to full for Scene 5*

*Cue* 13  **Frank** exits         (Page 23)
*Fade light to a single spot on Mary*

*Cue* 14  Telephone rings         (Page 23)
*Spot on telephone*

*Cue* 15  **Mary:** "... thinking our own thoughts"         (Page 24)
*Full stage lighting for Scene 6*

*Cue* 16  **Frank:** "... let's go and find our son."         (Page 28)
*Fade to Black-out*

# EFFECTS PLOT

### SCENE 1

*Cue* 1     The Curtains open. A moment later       (Page 1)
*Telephone rings several times then stops*

### SCENE 5

*Cue* 2     **Mary** moves upstage and sits       (Page 23)
*Telephone rings three times then stops*

www.ingramcontent.com/pod-product-compliance
Ingram Content Group UK Ltd.
Pitfield, Milton Keynes, MK11 3LW, UK
UKHW021821150726
7214IPUK00017B/250

9 780573 120817